How to Secure Investor Cash for Your Idea

20 Questions Smart Investors Ask Before Bankrolling Your Project (And How You Must Answer Them To Ensure Maximum Funding)

by Rob Gramer

Warning-Disclaimer: I wrote this report to provide information in regard to the subject matter covered. It is offered with the understanding that the publisher and the author are not liable for the misconception or misuse of the information provided.

Every effort has been made to make this report as complete and accurate as possible. The purpose of this report is to educate. The author and the publisher shall have neither liability nor responsibility to any person or entity with respect to any loss, damage, or injury caused or alleged to be caused directly or indirectly by the information contained in this report. No offer of investment is being made. The information presented herein is in no way intended as a substitute for legal counseling.

Go to www.inventionprep.com to learn how to start profiting off your idea in the next 30 days.

2

Inside:

Go to www.inventionprep.com to learn how to start profiting off your idea in the next 30 days.

3

Go to www.inventionprep.com to learn how to start profiting off your idea in the next 30 days.

4

How to Secure Investor Cash for Your Idea

20 questions smart investors ask before bankrolling your project (and how you must answer them to ensure maximum funding).

The report you are reading now contains the secrets to securing investor funding for your product, business or idea.

It doesn't matter if you don't have a finished product, a business plan, or even a prototype...even if it is nothing more than an idea in your head...the proven steps and systems outlined here will show you *exactly* what you must do and say to attract people who can finance your project.

My name is Rob Gramer. For the past few years I've worked for a law firm that specializes in applying for patents for inventors. My job is to talk to inventors and find out if their idea qualifies for a patent.

I'm uniquely qualified for this for two reasons:

Go to www.inventionprep.com to learn how to start profiting off your idea in the next 30 days.

5

First, my technical background. I hold a Bachelors of Science in mechanical engineering and have worked with big firms like Boeing, Lockheed Martin, Pratt and Whitney, Sikorsky, and the ultra secretive Defense Advanced Research Projects Agency.

Before that - while I was growing up - I was a chubby, introverted kid. Instead of making friends, I retreated into books and building things. Legos were my favorite toys. When the family lawn mower broke, I checked out a book from the library on how to fix it. I've fixed every appliance you can think of, rebuilt motorcycles, and have put additions on houses.

I could go on, but let's just say I enjoy designing and building things.

Second, my business background. As much as I love engineering and building things, the harsh truth is that you can only make so much of an income in that field. And since what I did was government contract work, when the contracts dry up...so does the work. The turning point for me came when I found out a buddy of mine was raking in almost $50,000 a year running a little bicycle taxi business. He had barely graduated high school, and at 21 had 5 people working for him, handing him anywhere from $50 to $200 a night just riding a bike.

At that point I vowed I would learn the business side of things, because that's where the real money is

Go to www.inventionprep.com to learn how to start profiting off your idea in the next 30 days.

6

at. Since then I've been involved in multiple businesses including, home electronics, construction, offshore bank account and second citizenship advice, tax accounting software, martial arts DVD's, weight loss plans, cookware, and on and on.

(The patent law firm was actually a client of mine before they hired me on full time, I was helping them with their online marketing efforts).

Because of these two sides of my background, I cannot only quickly understand how things work, I can also see why it could be valuable in the marketplace.

Anyways, working at the law firm has put me in the very interesting position of 1) Hearing all types of new ideas...and 2) Seeing how inventors fund these ideas to get them off the ground.

And what's really interested me the most are the cash-strapped inventors who talk investors into giving them tens of thousands of dollars...sometimes without a prototype, a business plan, or any sales whatsoever.

If you've ever wondered how some people seem to have the almost magical ability to raise cash, then this report is for you

Go to www.inventionprep.com to learn how to start profiting off your idea in the next 30 days.

7

I remember one guy who had a great idea for a website (because of confidentiality, I can't share with you the idea, but trust me when I said it was a good one). He went to a developer and was quoted $10,000 to build the website. $10,000.

This guy was in the midst of a divorce...had a young kid (with another on the way)...and was being downsized at work, but with the power of the idea alone...he talked investors into giving him not only the $10,000 to build the site...but another $20,000 to market it!

How did he do it? Today I will share with you those secrets. This report is divided into three parts:

1. First, I'll show you the most common questions investors ask inventors before loaning them money.
2. Next, I'll break those questions down into three categories (what the investors are really looking for).
3. And finally, I'll show you how to answer those questions (with successful examples), to maximize your chances of securing funding for your idea. And I'll give you an additional resource that will supercharge your chances for success once you are in front of investors (and another resource on HOW to find investors).

Enough of the preamble, let's get started.

Go to www.inventionprep.com to learn how to start profiting off your idea in the next 30 days.

8

Go to www.inventionprep.com to learn how to
start profiting off your idea in the next 30 days.

9

The 20 Questions

A big chunk of this list of questions came from an angel investor at a big New York City firm. The rest is assembled from personal meetings I've been in with investors.

Without further ado here are the twenty most common questions:

1. What is your competitive advantage?
2. What is your unfair advantage; the advantage no one else has or will have?
3. What was or will be your most important, early milestone?
4. How are you going to make money?
5. How do you know this is going to work?
6. Who are you and what have you done previously?
7. What do you need to make this successful and how are you going to get it?
8. Who is your first customer?
9. How will you get to 100 or 1,000 customers?
10. Who do you need to hire, when, and how are you going to recruit the right talent?
11. What's your business all about?
12. What's the barrier to entry for the competition?
13. What's going to stop big monster company in your space from copying you?
14. Why are you raising the money you want to raise?

Go to www.inventionprep.com to learn how to start profiting off your idea in the next 30 days.

10

15. How far does that money get you?

16. What's your marketing strategy?

17. What's the team look like? What are your backgrounds?

18. Who else have you spoken to?

19. How easily can you be copied?

20. Who are your competitors and how are you different?

We will dive into these questions shortly. But for now, realize that these questions can be broken up into three categories.

1. Questions about your idea, concept, or invention (what I call the "product")

2. Questions about how you'll design, manufacture, and sell the product (your "plan")

3. Questions about your skills and background (what I call "personal")

Product. Plan. Personal. I call these the **Three P's of Investor Funding**. Keep in mind that some of these questions overlap, and fall into more than one category. We'll be covering these questions from multiple angles.

Understanding how to answer them from these multiple angles, why investors ask the three P's, what they are looking for, and how to answer them is the difference between getting a big check and walking away empty handed.

Go to www.inventionprep.com to learn how to start profiting off your idea in the next 30 days.

11

The good news is, you don't have to ace ALL of these questions. You simply must convince an investor that you are competent in just ONE area (if all three, all the better, but it is not necessary).

For example,

- If you've built a time machine (your product), the investor won't care what your plan is or how successful you've been in the past. The product is so unique nothing else matters.
- If you can demonstrate a manufacturing process that will cut production cost of an expensive product in half (the plan), the product and you don't really matter.
- If you can show how you've been successful in the past (or just show great potential), investors may overlook shortcomings in the product and your plan.

Remember these three points. Investors can and will invest in your product, your plan, or you if just any one of them sounds like a great idea.

Now, let's get to the meat and potatoes of this report. What you need to say to secure funding. We'll begin with the "product" question and answers.

Go to www.inventionprep.com to learn how to start profiting off your idea in the next 30 days.

12

Part One: Product

"The most successful products solve a problem or save money."
- Billionaire investor Kevin O'Leary (quoted from the show "Shark Tank")

Out of the twenty questions, here are the ones that fall into the "product" category.

1. What is your competitive advantage?
2. What is your unfair advantage, the advantage no one else has or will have?
3. What's your business all about?
4. What's the barrier to entry for competition?
5. What's going to stop big monster company in your space from copying you?
6. How easily can you be copied?
7. Who are your competitors and how are you better/different?

Did you notice a pattern in these questions? If not, look again. All of them (except for question #3) have something in common.

Give up?

Look closely and you'll see all of these questions are framed NOT in the context of your product...but how it compares to your competition. Just look at the words: competitive advantage, unfair advantage, barrier to entry, copying you, better/different. The investors want to know how is your product/business/idea going to stack up to the competition.

This comes as a huge shock to many inventors.

Many inventors get so wrapped up in the inner workings of their invention, the type of material it is built with, the cool new features, or the code in the software, that they forget how to make it truly UNIQUE in the marketplace.

And while all of the "nuts and bolts" of the invention are important, it doesn't amount to a hill of beans if you can't stop the "big monster company" in the space from copying your idea. This can be a hard idea to wrap your head around, so let's see how some of the world's most profitable companies answer these questions:

In 1987, Austrian entrepreneur Dietrich Mateschitz invented Red Bull. Today, it is the world's best selling energy drink, selling 4.5 billion cans each year. How - in a span of less than twenty years - did this company go from nothing to dominating the world...while competing with companies like Coca Cola and Pepsi...who have dominated the soft drink market for the better part of a century?

By NOT being a soft drink.

Go to www.inventionprep.com to learn how to start profiting off your idea in the next 30 days.

14

If you've ever had a Red Bull, then you know it lacks the sweetness found in most soft drinks. To many people the sour, tangy taste of a Red Bull isn't bad, but it isn't good. But Red Bull doesn't compete on taste. Instead, they were the first widely marketed "drink" product claiming to increase energy via supplements and jacking up the caffeine (in fact, their tagline is "Red Bull gives you wings".)

This is their differentiation strategy.

By not competing on taste, and instead competing on energy they could declare themselves unique in a marketplace cluttered with "sweet" drinks. And since most soft drink products rely on taste (a Coke tastes different from Mountain Dew tastes different from Ginger Ale tastes different from Orange Soda...but all rely on some level of sweetness) they created a new category.

Energy drinks. NOT soft drinks.

Another good example is those little insulating sleeves you see wrapped around coffee cups. Do you know how people prevented burned fingers before those insulating sleeves were invented? Here are a few ways:

- Cups with handles (usually ceramic)
- Thermoses
- Styrofoam cups

Go to www.inventionprep.com to learn how to start profiting off your idea in the next 30 days.

15

But all of these presented a problem. Ceramic cups are heavy. Thermoses are expensive to make. Styrofoam cups are flimsy. And mass coffee distribution requires cheap, sturdy solutions. Paper cups are cheap but allow too much heat to pass through.

The solution?

Corrugated coffee cup sleeves. The extra space allows the heat to dissipate (so you can grab the cup and not burn yourself). Let's revisit a few of our product questions and see how coffee cup sleeves stack up to the competition.

1. What is your competitive advantage?

Coffee cup sleeves are cheaper to manufacture than ceramic and thermoses. And when combined with existing paper cups, are stronger than Styrofoam.

2. What is your unfair advantage, the advantage no one else has or will have?

Coffee cup sleeves can be used with existing technology (paper cups), therefore we won't need to reinvent the wheel. The technology is also protected by a patent (patent #5,425,497), so the unfair advantage is competitors cannot use it without (usually paid for) permission.

3. Who are your competitors and how are you better/different?

Go to www.inventionprep.com to learn how to start profiting off your idea in the next 30 days.

16

Cheaper than ceramic mugs and thermoses. Easy to use with existing paper cups. Stronger than Styrofoam.

Now obviously this is a very narrow discussion on the merits of coffee cup sleeves versus other options. But it shows how a different solution to the problem can result in a very good idea. And in this particular situation, those sleeves are found in every coffee shop around the country.

But does your product have to be different to attract investors? Of course not. There are plenty of thriving businesses and ideas that sell the exact same product and can compete successfully for a profit. How do they do it? By HOW they present the product...NOT what the product actually is.

Go to www.inventionprep.com to learn how to start profiting off your idea in the next 30 days.

17

Part Two: Plan or Process

"If one does not know to which port one is sailing, no wind is favorable."
\- Lucius Annaeus Seneca

Out of the twenty questions, here are the ones that fall into the "plan and process" category.

1. What is your competitive advantage?
2. What was or will be your most important, early milestone?
3. How are you going to make money?
4. What do you need to make this successful and how are you going to get it?
5. Who is your first customer?
6. How will you get to 100 or 1,000 customers?
7. Who do you need to hire, when, and how are you going to recruit the right talent?
8. What's the barrier to entry for the competition?
9. What's going to stop big monster company in your space from copying you?
10. How far does that money get you?
11. What's your marketing strategy?
12. Who are your competitors and how are you better/different?

I live in citrus country in South Florida. You can find an orange tree on almost every block. The middle of the state is covered with miles upon miles of

Go to www.inventionprep.com to learn how to start profiting off your idea in the next 30 days.

18

orange trees. Yet our supermarkets are filled with orange juice shipped in from Brazil.

Why is this?

Cheap labor. Up to 40% cheaper by some reports. Multiply this by thousands of gallons of orange juice and you're talking big money. Because of this, it is cheaper to grow, squeeze, and ship orange juice from Brazil to Florida than it is to use homegrown oranges!

In this case, the profit isn't in the product itself (the orange juice is basically the same). The profit is in the process of using cheap labor in Brazil to cut production costs.

If you can prove that your plan or process will make or save money - even if you have a ho hum product - then you are well on your way to persuading investors to fund your venture.

Let's look at another example. With a value of over $166 billion dollars, and control of over 40% of the soft drink market, Coca Cola sits firmly atop as the most powerful soft drink brand in the world.

But there are plenty of competitors out there. Pepsi, Danone, Nestea, etc. How do they maintain dominance? Simple. They control the distribution channels, the planes, trains, and trucks that deliver soft drinks to supermarkets, convenience stores, and gas stations. They even pay for premium placement in supermarket aisles.

Go to www.inventionprep.com to learn how to start profiting off your idea in the next 30 days.

19

It is nearly impossible to gain any traction in the soft drink market unless you go through the distribution chain Coca Cola built.

So their answer to a competitive advantage is...we own the distribution chain. Even if they sell a subpar product (which many people agree Pepsi is better), they can still dominate their market because of the distribution chain.

Now of course not everybody has access to millions of workers willing to slave away for pennies or a distribution chain built up over the last century. So how can the average Joe claim a plan or process that will have investors chomp at the bit?

The answer lies in knowing what your customer wants...

This is how Dominos Pizza dominated the pizza market in the early 80's. Their target customer was hungry, impatient, and broke college kids who didn't care if food was healthy or not. So Dominos hit them between the eyeballs with an offer they couldn't refuse "Fresh, hot pizza delivered in 30 minutes or less, guaranteed".

It worked so well the founder Tom Monaghan ended up selling Domino for roughly one billion dollars.

Go to www.inventionprep.com to learn how to start profiting off your idea in the next 30 days.

20

Dominos had a valuable process. Cook and deliver pizzas within 30 minutes or it's free. Notice they didn't say anything about healthy. Notice they didn't say anything about good tasting. Just get it there and make sure it's hot. This is something NO other pizza joint offered at the time (and it put Dominos on the map while other successful, long established pizza restaurants closed their doors).

In case you missed that lesson, this is how the "little guy" can compete with market dominators. Know what your customer wants (more than anything else)...create a plan or process to give them what they want...and then deliver.

But what if you have a ho-hum product AND no good plan or process to make it succeed? In that case you must convince investors of your PERSONAL assets that will help the project succeed.

Go to www.inventionprep.com to learn how to start profiting off your idea in the next 30 days.

21

Part Three: Personal (YOU!)

"Most of the important things in the world have been accomplished by people who have kept on trying when there seemed to be no hope at all."
- Dale Carnegie

Out of the twenty questions, here are the ones that fall into the "personal" category.

1. What is your competitive advantage?
2. What is your unfair advantage; the advantage no one else has or will have?
3. How do you know this is going to work?
4. Who are you and what have you done previously?
5. What's your business all about?
6. Why are you raising the money you want to raise?
7. What's the team look like? What are your backgrounds?
8. Who else have you spoken to?
9. How easily can you be copied?
10. Who are your competitors and how are you different?

If you are trying to secure investor funding for a new cancer cure it would definitely help if you are a doctor with extensive training in treating cancer. But how long does that take?

Go to www.inventionprep.com to learn how to start profiting off your idea in the next 30 days.

22

There's college and medical school, years of 18 hour days in residency, and tons of tests. That's a huge time investment. I don't have that kind of time to wait, and I don't think you do either.

I think it was General George S. Patton who said, *"A good plan, violently executed now, is better than a perfect plan next week."*

And out of the three sections, unless you outright lie about your credentials (which you shouldn't do), this one is the hardest to create out of thin air. You may be able to come up with a better mouse trap, or a unique way of doing things, but you shouldn't lie about your experience.

But you still need good answers for these questions. So start by looking into your personal history to see how it is relevant to making this project succeed. What is your background? What school did you attend? Who did you work for? What did you do as a child?

The answers to these types of questions may just convince an investor that you are the right person for the job. I'll give you a personal example.

When it was time to apply for college, I didn't really have much to show. Antisocial and rebellious in high school, I didn't volunteer, participate in clubs, or play sports. And my 3.0 grade point average was nothing to brag about. To boot, my lack of respect for

Go to www.inventionprep.com to learn how to start profiting off your idea in the next 30 days.

23

authority got me in trouble with the law on a few occasions.

So how - with ok grades, no school involvement, and a (just for the record, non-violent and non-drug related) arrest record did I get accepted to ALL of the schools I applied for? In a highly competitive major like mechanical engineering?

The answer reveals how you prove yourself in almost any situation (even coaxing money out of investors). Here's what I did. I wrote letters to everyone who was in charge of admissions. Presidents, Vice Presidents, Deans, teachers, etc. I was honest about my shortcomings. And then I explained why my background was unique and beneficial to them, and why I should be accepted into their program. It went a little bit like this

Dear (Person),

"On paper, I do not look like the ideal student. I'll admit my grades are ok, I have no extracurricular activity to speak of, and - frankly - I've had some run in's with the law.

However, I have something to offer that makes me a more qualified candidate for admission into your mechanical engineering program than any other student you will come across. And that is simply my passion for making things."

Go to www.inventionprep.com to learn how to start profiting off your idea in the next 30 days.

24

I then went on to explain how my favorite toys as a child were things I could build, like legos. How I spent my youth taking apart and rebuilding remote control cars, bicycles, and lawn mowers. How I added a car port, porch, and other additions to the house.

THIS showed promise in their eyes. And that one letter was how I secured a slot in every engineering program I applied to, DESPITE my less than stellar academic record.

This is key - you must show investors how YOU are relevant to the project at hand. You don't need outside credentials. And you definitely don't need to be perfect. You must simply show how your unique background and past experience will make this venture succeed. Do that and you'll be well on your way securing the trust (and financial backing) of investors.

At the beginning of this report I promised to show you how to supercharge your chances for success once you are in front of investors. I will now fulfill on that promise.

The Golden Rule to Securing Investor Funds

If you read between the lines of these twenty questions, you'll see investors want to know what your unique advantage is compared to any and every other product or service out there.

Go to www.inventionprep.com to learn how to start profiting off your idea in the next 30 days.

25

In other words, what kind of **LEVERAGE** do you have?

One dictionary definition of leverage is:

> the power or ability to act or to influence people, events, decisions, etc. **Example***: Being the only industry in town gave the company considerable lever in its union negotiations.* **Synonyms:** advantage, strength, weight, clout, pull.

And that's really the key for ALL of the questions no matter what category they fall in.

- What's the leverage in your product?
- What's the leverage in your plan?
- What's the leverage in you?

By answering the 20 questions laid out in this report, you will precisely define that leverage. Present this to the right investors and you will prove to them that you...your product...and your plan are worth investing in.

Go to www.inventionprep.com to learn how to start profiting off your idea in the next 30 days.

26

Did You Know There Is A Way To Raise Funding For Your Idea That DOES NOT Involve Giving Away Equity To Investors?

Everything you need to convince investors to fund your idea is hidden within you, your plan, or your product.

The difficult (and time consuming part) is digging out the most persuasive elements...and...presenting them in a way that is appealing to investors (who are actively looking for good ideas to invest in).

That's where I come in. I help people who have ideas and inventions (just like you) create presentation to persuade investors to back your ideas.

And if you're not ready to present to investors just yet, I can show you:

- How to save thousands of dollars on legal fees while patenting your invention
- How to find designers and engineers to create your ideas on paper and in real life (from sketches to prototypes, to mass manufacturing) quicker than you ever dreamed possible
- And, how to get all the money you need WITHOUT investors...usually within 30 days (AND you get to keep ALL your equity)

Go to www.inventionprep.com to learn how to start profiting off your idea in the next 30 days.

27

Most people think it takes a major investment of time and money to get their ideas off the ground.

Now you can start profiting from your ideas and inventions in as little as 30 days.

If you'd like me to help, just send an email to Rob@inventionprep.com and we'll take it from there.

Go to www.inventionprep.com to learn how to start profiting off your idea in the next 30 days.

28

Awesome Free Bonuses!

Visit www.inventionprep.com for free instant access to more free cool stuff like...

- Personal feedback from licensed patent professionals, engineers, and experienced marketers on how to protect, create, and sell your idea.
- How to save thousands on legal fees to protect your idea
- Quickly and cheaply create prototypes and final products (in days instead of weeks or months)
- Profit from your idea as quick as humanely possible...usually inside 30 days

Just go to www.inventionprep.com for instant access.

Go to www.inventionprep.com to learn how to start profiting off your idea in the next 30 days.

29

Appendix A: The Questions

1. What is your competitive advantage?
2. What is your unfair advantage; the advantage no one else has or will have?
3. What was or will be your most important, early milestone?
4. How are you going to make money?
5. How do you know this is going to work?
6. Who are you and what have you done previously?
7. What do you need to make this successful and how are you going to get it?
8. Who is your first customer?
9. How will you get to 100 or 1,000 customers?
10. Who do you need to hire, when, and how are you going to recruit the right talent?
11. What's your business all about?
12. What's the barrier to entry for the competition?
13. What's going to stop big monster company in your space from copying you?
14. Why are you raising the money you want to raise?
15. How far does that money get you?
16. What's your marketing strategy?
17. What's the team look like? What are your backgrounds?
18. Who else have you spoken to?
19. How easily can you be copied?
20. Who are your competitors and how are you different?

Go to www.inventionprep.com to learn how to start profiting off your idea in the next 30 days.

30

Go to www.inventionprep.com to learn how to start profiting off your idea in the next 30 days.

31

www.ingramcontent.com/pod-product-compliance
Lightning Source LLC
Chambersburg PA
CBHW070732180526
45167CB00004B/1717